The Ashes of Spent Affirmations

Ganapathy Mahalingam

(Second Edition)

ISBN-13: 978-0998098555 (Pensive Muse Books)
ISBN-10: 0998098558

Second Edition

DEDICATION

This book is dedicated, in fond memory, to my parents, Lakshmi and G. Mahalingam, who made all my affirmations possible by enabling my first affirmation.

CONTENTS

ACKNOWLEDGMENTS

not a word in the **world**
the con in a **con**cept
or the or in the**or**y
makes the but of a contri**but**ion
stand in any under**stand**ing

1 THE LITTLE WAVE

THE LITTLE WAVE ASKED A ?

the little wave asked a question
as it bounced and swirled
leapt and curled
and then burst in glee
what am I, but a sun kissed crest
of life from 'neath the sea
deep down I have struggled
in gurgle wildernesses
where monsters moan
in eerie eternity
flaps of tail
and fins aflail
have lashed my face and fleed
my head was caught
my neck was wrung
as I floundered 'midst some weed
till a warm ballast
of some force
lifted me, and I was freed
freed to surge my way atop
and sing my liberty

2 GRACE

What is Grace and why do we need it?

In Christianity, there is a calling to abide in the Divine ("Abide in me" from the "Vine Sermon" - John 15: 1-8).

In Islam, there is a calling to be a Muslim (one who subjugates oneself to the will of Allah, the act of Islam).

In the *Sanātana* Dharma (aka Hinduism), there is a calling to become one (merge) with *Brahman* (the Divine) through Yoga.

If we are to fulfill these callings...we need the Grace that the Divine bestows upon us...the Grace to know when we are abiding in the Divine and not anywhere else...the Grace to know when we are subjugating ourselves to the will of Allah and not the will of our own selves and other human beings...the Grace to know when we have merged with *Brahman*...without this Grace, we will not know if we have fulfilled our callings, and will have nothing to guide us in our quest!

Callings, Grace and what hides the Divine Essence from Us

In all the great religious traditions of the world, we encounter significant callings that are revealed to us. These callings are easy to grasp and understand. The difficulty that emerges, is knowing when we have attained the callings. How does one know that they are abiding in Christ and not someone, or something else? How does one know that they are subjugating themselves to the will of Allah and not some human being? How does one know that they have become one with the Divine? This special knowledge, where we know we have attained our calling, can come only from Divine grace! The Hindus knew, a long time ago, that discovering this Divine essence was no easy task. They explained that the process was complicated, with many sheaths and limitations that prevented us from getting very close to the Divine. The *Advaitins*, or non-dualists, believe that the individual Self, *Ātman*, and the Supreme Divine Being, *Brahman*, are one and the same. The *Ātman* is covered in layers or sheaths, much like an onion, that prevents us from realizing its Divine essence.

There are 5 such sheaths or *koshas*.

Annamayakosha (this is the sheath created by the gross body that is sustained by food, the limitations of our physiology)

Prānamayakosha (this is the sheath created by our vital body: the breathing, digestion and blood circulation)

Manomayakosha (this is the sheath created by our mind and its vagaries: emotions, doubts and volition)

Vijñānamayakosha (this the sheath created by our intellect: our reasoning and decision making)

Ānandamayakosha (this is the sheath created by our bliss and false complacency that we have discovered the Divine essence)

In addition to these *koshas*, there are limitations or *upādhis* that prevent us from realizing the Divine essence of the *Ātman*. These *upādhis* are individual and collective. The individual *upādhis* are a result of our *koshas*. The collective *upādhis* are a result of our social and religious beliefs. A poetic description of an *upādhi* is visualizing the Divine, *Brahman*, descending into water. The *upādhi* of the water makes *Brahman* a fish. Similarly, our waking, dream and dreamless sleep states of consciousness create *upādhis* that hide the Divine essence from us. When we overcome our *koshas*, or sheaths, and our *upādhis*, or limitations, we get close to attaining the Divine essence.

The *paramārtha* or Divine essence is hidden from us by the five *koshas* and the *upādhis*. The *annamayakosha* or the physiological sheath sustained by food is transcended by *āsanas*. The *prānamayakosha* or the vital sheath of breathing, blood circulation and digestion, is transcended by *prānāyāma*. The *manomayakosha* or mental sheath is transcended by *pratyahāra* and *dhāranā*. The *vijñānamayakosha* or intellectual sheath is transcended by *dhyāna* and the *ānandamayakosha* or sheath of bliss is transcended by *apavāda*. In addition to transcending these sheaths that hide the *paramārtha*, one must overcome the *upādhis* of the states of waking (which is *nāma* and *rūpa*), dreaming (which is the *vikshepa shakti* of *māyā*) and dreamless deep sleep (which is the *āvarana shakti* of *māyā*). Once the *koshas* and *upādhis* are overcome, one gets a glimpse of the ultimate reality.

This call to abide in the Divine, which is also found in Christianity, is beautifully captured in the *mahāvākyas* or great sayings of the Vedas.

These great sayings can be arranged in a majestic progression.

Prajñānam Brahma (*Rig* Veda) (All consciousness is *Brahman*)

Ayam Ātmā Brahma (*Atharva* Veda) (My Self is *Brahman*)

Aham Brahmāsmi (*Yajur* Veda) (I am going to abide in *Brahman*) (this is an unconventional translation)

Tat Tvam Asi (*Sama* Veda) (You (should) abide in That (*Brahman*)) (this is also an unconventional translation)

In a slightly nuanced reading of *asmi* and *asi* in Sanskrit, the alignment of Christianity and Hinduism is revealed. When you realize that the Sanskrit word *asi*, the Hindi word *vāsi*, and the German word *dasein*, are all cognates for expressing the concept of 'dwelling,' the call to abide, or dwell, in the Divine becomes clearer. In this common calling, the great religious traditions of the world can find peace!

Om tat sat Brahmārpanamastu! (May that truth be dedicated to *Brahman*)

(From the presentation notes on above topic at Concordia College in Moorhead, Minnesota on April 16, 2012)

The nuanced reading takes its cue from the root *as*, which is translated as, 'to be'.

Ganesh Darshan

I presented a talk at the Memorial Union Gallery at North Dakota State University based on an art piece I had on display in the Create...Collect Faculty Show titled, 'Ganesh Darshan.' The provocative piece suggests that the Hindu deity Ganesha is really the faculty offered by our inner ear, which serves as our link to the divine voice, our voice of conscience, our source of thought, our source of beginnings, and our resonance with the primordial universal vibration, characterized by the Hindu symbol of 'Aum.'

I had created a series of these digital art pieces some years ago, that I now like to call...the Ganesh Darshan Series. It provides us insight into what Ganesha really is...our inner ear. In the art work, one can see the form of Ganesha...& the Tamil symbol for 'Aum'...makes us wonder what Rama, Krishna, Lakshmi and Saraswati really are...are they deities and divinities in our bodies that guide our faculties?...such is the poetry of Hinduism!

Let's look at Ganesha...

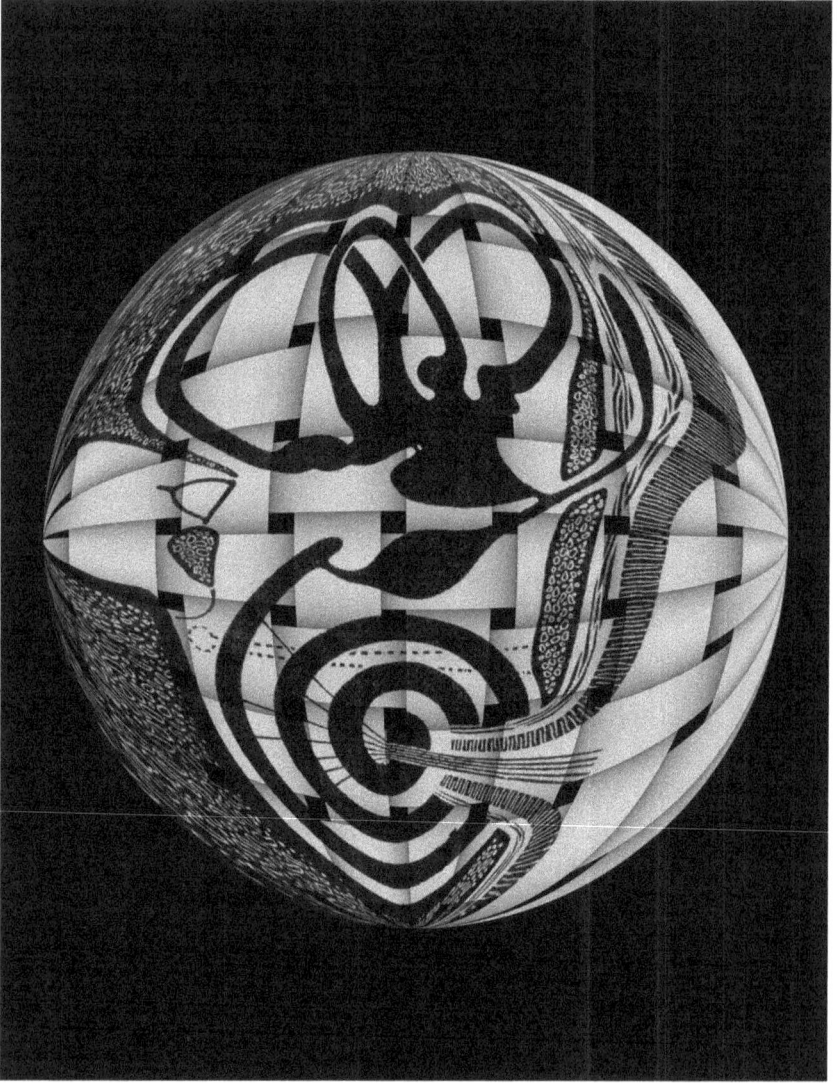

On Being a Vegetarian

Often, I am called upon to rationalize why I am a vegetarian. Points of contention have been the drinking of milk, and the eating of milk products such as butter, ghee, curds, yogurt and cheese. The acceptance of eggs in cakes, muffins, croissants and other baked products have also been called into question. These days you cannot escape taking eggs even when having ice cream. So, how does one form an ethical basis for one's diet?

I have come up with the following as an answer:

The driving force behind being a vegetarian is not killing the source of your food. So with non-destructive harvesting, when you harvest cereals, the plants are not killed; when you harvest fruits and vegetables, the plants are not killed; even rhizomes and tubers, if properly harvested and replanted, need not end up in the killing of the plants; milk and milk products are also acceptable since the cow is not killed in the process of milking it; eggs (presumably not fertilized) are also acceptable since the hen is not killed when the eggs are collected. If one uses this test of not killing the source of one's food, it gives one enough of a dietary range to meet nutritional needs.

If we consume food without killing the source of our food, then we can rationalize what can be an ethical basis for our diet. We will still be left with the option of enjoying most of the foods we have come to enjoy in various cultures.

3 GREAT SAYINGS

An alternate reading of the essence of the Vedas - the "*mahāvākyas*" or "great sayings"

The essence or wisdom of the *Sanatana* Dharma (aka Hinduism) is embodied in the four Vedas. In each of the four Vedas, the *Rig*, *Yajur*, *Sama* and *Atharva* Vedas (the traditional hierarchy), there is a "*mahāvākya*" or "great saying" that captures an essence of the whole belief system.

The four *mahāvākyas* or great sayings are:

prajñānam Brahma (*Rig* Veda)
ayam ātmā Brahma (*Atharva* Veda)
aham Brahmāsmi (*Yajur* Veda)
tat tvam asi (*Sama* Veda)

While there may be no innate hierarchy in the Vedas, and even though traditionally one creates a hierarchy based on chronological development, there could be postulated a new hierarchy (as above) of the four Vedas based on the *mahāvākyas*, based on an alternate reading of what the *mahāvākyas* mean.

Let us consider the following interpretations:

prajñānam Brahma: "Universal wisdom (is) *Brahman* (universal

Consciousness)." This is an observation that is rooted in wonder when considering the cosmos and everything in it. This reflects the attitude and spirit of the *Rig* Veda.

ayam ātmā Brahma "My Self (is) *Brahman*." This is a realization that comes subsequent to the wonder and the observation of *prajñānam Brahma*. The humility in the realization is in the reference to "*ayam*" or "my" with the objective tone. This reflects the attitude and spirit of the *Atharva* Veda, and is the voice of the *Atharvan*, or priest.

aham Brahmāsmi: "I am going to dwell in (be, abide in) *Brahman*." This is an assertion, with the resolute tone, of one who has realized the Self. This reflects the attitude and spirit of the *Yajur* Veda, and is the voice of the enlightened individual.

tat tvam asi: "You dwell in (abide) in that (*Brahman*)." This is a directive, a teaching, with the imperative tone. This reflects the attitude and spirit of the *Sama* Veda, and is the voice of the teacher or guru wishing to share the experience of enlightenment.

The hierarchy, as arranged above, now progresses from observation, to realization, to resolution (as applied to oneself), to teaching (others), in one majestic sequence. This is possible by reading "*asmi*" as "am going to be, or, going to dwell in" (resolution) and "*asi*" as "be, or, dwell in" (directive). These Sanskrit words are cognate with "*vāsi*" or "dweller."

The beauty that emerges from this system is difficult to ignore. Hinduism has come to some grief due to the traditional readings and interpretations of the *mahāvākyas*. This reading may provide an alternative, open doors, build bridges, and reveal the elegant grace embodied in the Vedas.

4 FIGURE/GROUND

The perception of a figure and a ground against which the figure emerges (the background) is inherent and unavoidable in perception with the senses and the mind. It is a pre-condition to the registering of any qualia or qualitative aspects of perception. Minds often alternate between the perception of the figure and that of the ground, making the ground the figure in the alternate perception.

The perception of the figure, and the alternate perception of the ground, are like striking the faces of the two-faced drum of Shiva, the *damaru*. Things are brought into existence (made figural) and things dissolve into the background (made ground) in a dance of creation and destruction, to the beating of Shiva's drum. The creation and dissolution of all that is perceived, which is the creation and dissolution of our worlds from moment to moment through the dance of Shiva, is the alternate emergence of figures and grounds in one's perception with the senses and the mind.

In images of architecture, the mind alternates between the perception of a building and a landscape. This figure/ground perception is not confined to the visual sense, but applies to perception with all our senses and the mind.

What if the basis for all that we perceive as figural and real...so that the real *ex sists* (stands out) against a (back) ground...and the corresponding search for the ground state of all things real...is the vestige of this hard-wired trait of perception that we have as humans. What if we always perceive with this figure/ground filter, when we perceive with our minds? This may be the greatest *upādhi* of them all, giving rise to concepts of ground state, source, etc. and its differentiation from the self. Is Nature the figure, and Consciousness the ground? Is *Ātman* the figure, and *Brahman* the ground? Do they alternate as our focus in our pursuit of enlightenment? Is enlightenment then, the insight that there is no figure or ground, but a unity of the two? Such an insight would have to overcome the figure/ground filter that is intrinsic to perception with the senses and the mind. This may be a key aspect of the subtle *kārana upādhi*, the final limitation that has to be transcended in enlightenment.

In the *Advaitic* tradition, when we see the figure, it is *māyā* (not that)...when we see the ground, it is *māyā* (not that)...and when we say *neti, neti* (not thus, not thus...my translation)...the figure and ground dissolve into unity.

5 TIME AND SPACE

What does Time measure? Or, what do we measure, when we measure Time?

When we measure using a ruler, we know what we are measuring is an inorganic or organic object, because that is what we put the ruler against to make our measurement. When we run a clock, what is it that we are putting it against, that we are measuring?

We can tell time has passed, only when there is a reference that stands still, or moves relatively slower than the time that has passed. We mark time by observing or recording the states of changing physical (inorganic) matter, changing organic matter, or changing mental worlds. If inorganic matter stood still, if organic matter stood still, and our minds stood still, there would be no flowing of Time, there would be nothing to mark (or measure) its passage.

Ever since the dissipation that began with the Big Bang (one of the theories of cosmology)...the cosmos has been transformed by the flow of energy that alters the states of the various things that exist. These states are perceived by sentient beings...who structure them in a sequence...before, now, after...a process that marks and gives rise to Time. So a measurement of Time is really a measurement (or is it a recording or marking) of the changing state of the universe, which in turn, is a measure of the energy transforming it.

The primary function of Architecture is to mark Time...to allow Time to exist (to stand out against its own passing) and to pass. Without a changing architectural substrate...how can we tell of one thing being of a particular time...and another thing being of another time. Even in our mental experiences we have a substrate that is the architecture of our minds...our *samskāra*...that which has created our minds...the mental passage of time...from memories to hopes...plays out against this *samskāra*.

We all know that clocks tell the time...but what is it that they measure?...Einstein gave us the relationship between matter and energy...what is the relationship between matter and time? An answer will close out a loop of enlightenment!

On the Passage of Time

In order for Time to pass something must resist the flowing of Time...something must stand still or flow relatively slower than Time...this is our sense of Self...that which endures...enduring means that a duration is involved...duration that may stand still or move slower than Time...a close reading of Bergson and the notion of Self, as in *Advaita*, will let us see...why, in order for Time to pass...something must stand still or move slower than Time...

I ask this question of all my students in the seminar class on the Architecture of India...what if you are standing in the entrance to the Taj Mahal at sunrise...when there is no reference for chronological time (sounds of cars, buses, aircraft overhead)...what time is it at the Taj?...is your experience rooted in the 16th century or the 21st century...a little bit more pondering... and we realize why we mark Time with materials and technology...or as Einstein would have it, events in a Space-Time continuum...does Time slice Space or does Space slice Time?...material culture is an external reference to the passage of Time...far different from the sense of Time as known by one who endures...

The Linear Arrow of Time folded into a Peano Curve

The concept of cause and effect has created a linear model of Time...Time's arrow...this unraveling of Time, like a ball of string, requires infinite space. If the space is confined, as in our skull, like the brain, the linear arrow of Time folds to pack itself within the finite space. This is like a Peano curve...the curious situation that arises, is when there are short circuits...in space...that tangle the linear unfolding of Time's arrow...or is it Time's ball of string (like Ariadne's)...these are links in between the folding/unfolding Peano curve...which, in the theory of networks...creates small worlds...not the expansive, infinite world that is required for the unfolding of Time's arrow.

When the short circuiting happens in space, what happens to cause and effect and the linear model...and entropy?...this is why feedback systems...which may be different from short-circuited systems...and non-linear systems have fascinated scientists. Time may unfold...if it does so in finite space...say, within effective system boundaries...there are chances for it to become entangled and present itself to alternate readings...

Permeable Densities

In a recent class discussion, a student suggested that space is an absolute, and is a container for all things that exist. I then posed a question asking him why, just as there is room in a partially-filled box, there were no empty pockets of space with no matter in them, because zones of vacuum do not exist naturally. One could counter with an argument that when we move to microscopic subatomic levels of matter, there seem to be empty pockets of space between the molecules and atoms. Only now, the space is held within the matter, not matter held within the space, which acts as a container! What if there is no empty space, only contiguous matter in which space is entrapped! Space, then, would always be contained by 'vessels' of matter, varying in density, which are contiguous. What if, like a precious and vulnerable child, space is always contained and held within matter! Contiguous containers of matter, containing space! Now, what would this world of permeable densities mean to the modeling of energy transfer?

6 SENSING

The Eye of the Beholder

At any given moment, the universe is being perceived by billions of sentient beings (including humans). There is no coincidence of the 'locus' (that is, the spatial location) of these perceptions. For example, no two sets of eyes of human beings see the world at the same time from the same location (except maybe, curiously through the one 'eye' of a camera transmitting 'live', an artificial device).

There could be a synchronicity of all the perceptions (this would assume a disengaged clock (mechanical, electronic or even atomic)) giving rise to a notion of absolute Time that goes on independent of the perceptions. There could not be...coining a new use for a word here perhaps...a '**syntopy**'...a coincidence of spatial locations of the perceptions.

This challenges the notion that we could consider discussing a 'one common world' when all our perceptions have different spatial loci (not to mention mental loci). What do we actually share? This spatial distribution of sentience probably began with the origin of the universe...say in a Big Bang...and has continued since. How can we ever see through another's eyes (though there may be clever electronic devices that get us close)?

This is why, designers and architects, who work on spatial problems, use abstract representations, so that they have **a realm of syntopy** in which they can address a 'common world'...and perhaps why the ancients stumbled upon Geometry, as an abstract realm...which in the words of the architect, Louis Kahn...provided the common ground of agreement between men (and of course, women).

The Five Elements and the Five Senses

I saw a comment on a friend's wall on Facebook that prompted me to write this note. The ancients had this system of primal elements, called the *panchabhuta* in ancient Sanskrit: ether, air (wind), fire, water and earth (material). What many of us may not realize is how closely this classification of elements is related to our perceptual world, delivered to us by our senses. This is the hierarchy that we should understand in terms of relationships between the five senses and the five elements:
ether (hearing)
air (hearing, touch)
fire (hearing, touch, seeing)
water (hearing, touch, seeing and tasting)
earth (hearing, touch, seeing, tasting and smelling)

Considering an element and the sensory perception(s) related to it, if you have a sensory perception of one of the elements that is later in the hierarchy, then it is due to contamination, for example, if water smells, it may have been polluted with earth. Similarly, if a fire smells, it is because some earth (material) was burned.

Most Architecture is an ordering of all these elements, and thereby, the sensory perceptions related to them, which, together, gives us our experience of the built environment.

Every dawn, India's spirit awakens, and in myriads of ways, throughout the day, seeks its forms of expression. The unrelenting pursuit of divinity, with all its pain and purity, resolves itself in the splendor of the eye. In *tadanubhuti* and *tādātmyata*, everything dissolves into one experience and one soul, through performance by the spirit.

In the whispering of the ether
The ear is awakened
In the caress of the breeze

You are touched
In the surge of the flame
The eye is kindled
In the sipping of water
The tongue is quenched
And from the rain-drenched earth
The fragrant spirit is set free
This is the dance of the *panchabhutas*
The five elements that evoke
The five senses of the inner spirit
Ātman

Cotelydon

Footsteps on the fallen snow
Footsteps of an invisible flow
Hear them like the softer sound
Of one hand clapping
A forehead blow

Tears that fall down a face
At a running
Not a walking pace
Feel them like a seaside splash
Washing with a liquid grace

Thoughts that linger like a smell
Thoughts you wish you could quell
Stay much longer than you want
Wondering what it means to dwell

Laughter that tries to cleanse
A troubled heart, beating intense
Feel the murmur in the smile
Bringing poise and a balanced sense

Anger like a searing heat
Blinds you to things that cheat
Feel it burn into your bone
And wonder why it does repeat

Feel these things as silent sprouts
That thrust towards the sun
Feel them as a nascent nudge
In the mind's cotelydon

The Dance of the Afferent and the Efferent in Creative Media

At the gallery talk in connection with the display of the historical collection of drawings, an interesting idea was put forth about whether drawing was a process of 'output,' or a process of 'input' for a curious activity called 'thinkering.' In meditating upon this concept, it struck me that all media used for creative activities, be it clay thrown on a potter's wheel, or the use of paint on canvas, or a musical instrument, provide for this rapidly oscillating dance of the afferent and the efferent. Our neural system is described as a "closed loop" system of sensations, decisions, and reactions that engage the world around us. This process is carried out through the activity of afferent neurons, interneurons, and efferent neurons. This oscillating dance can happen at varying speeds, in varying cadences, and with syncopated patterns. A master of a creative activity is one who is of a clear enough mind, where there is an awareness of when the activity in the bodymind is afferent, that is, when it draws in the world, when the mind mediates the world in perception, and when the body is in its efferent phase, that is, acts on the world. This dance happens in cycles, like an endless waltz, transforming the world creatively. The power of a creative medium is in how it enables the afferent and the efferent, the kinds of cadences between them, the patterns that can be created, and the ability to achieve coherence in the process. Learning how to dance like this, evokes the cosmic dancer, whom the Hindus know as Nataraja, the lord of the dance.

7 AN ARCHITECTURAL JOURNEY

Architectural design is a journey that starts with unlimited possibilities and evolves through design decisions that reflect specificity with minimal tolerances. Life is like architectural design...it starts with unlimited possibilities and evolves through specific experiences and achievements. Each one's life is an architectural journey.

The Morality of Specificity and the Tragedy of Architecture

A student postulated that it was the student's purpose, through delineation, to evoke the imagination of spaces with ambiguity, and not make an attempt at portraying something that would indicate specificity. In light of this position, it struck me that this was contrary to the whole existential enterprise, which was predicated on 'standing out' (*ex sistare* in Latin: the figure) presumably against 'the other' (the ground). Individuation and specificity characterize the moral dimension of life. Making choices, and being responsible for choices, form the backbone of morality. The tragedy of architecture is that you have to build something specific. The environment that we live in, the environment that we learn from, and the environment that we perceive, are all the result of very specific decisions or processes. The people who made these decisions have the moral obligation for the consequences of the decisions. Wanting to abdicate specificity for ambiguity, is an abandonment of the moral life. It is easy to create architectural drawings that evoke the experience of ambiguous spaces. It is unforgiving to attempt to portray specificity in an architectural delineation or rendering. Often the exquisite pain in portraying an exacting specificity is passed up with an ambiguous compromise. It is moral to try to be specific. It is not easy to be moral.

Taking What We Can…

In writing about the life force (*élan vital*), Bergson envisioned a vital force coursing through matter taking from it what it can. In Western civilization this has become the spirit surging to manifest itself in the material, consuming vast amounts of energy in the process. The entropy in transforming material, limits what can be done in the future, often in irreversible ways. The need for the spirit to *ex sist* in the material and not just be of itself is a philosophical need. Should this be re-evaluated? The earth has a lot of material resources, a limited pool of non-renewable energy resources, and the potential of unlimited renewable energy resources. By regulating what materials we choose to manifest our spirit in, we can change the future course of civilizations dramatically. We may also be able to balance our energy resources with the demands for what is needed to transform material. What are the material and energy demands for a sufficient manifestation of the human spirit? Can we manifest the full vibrancy of the human spirit with a limited palette of materials and energy resources? Soon this may not be a choice, but an imperative!

Cuts Like a Knife

When one ponders a simple operation such as cutting, one has to think about what came first: the desire to perform the operation of cutting, which necessitated the invention of a cutting implement, or, the invention of a cutting implement that made the operation of cutting possible. What implements have we yet to invent if we started with desired operations and then sought the tools or implements to perform those operations? The Greeks pondered the atomic structure of matter because they could cut through an apple! Have we invented all the tools for our desires? What will these tools reveal about the universe? What irreversible operations might these tools unleash upon the processes of the universe? What have these tools enabled that were not the desired operations that were the cause of their invention? What have we implemented? Cuts like a knife...

Towards an Architecture of Silence

The eye is a silent place. The mind's eye, however, is different. In the mind's eye, there is an acoustic chatter, the vehicle of desire, that adds a layer of complexity to the silent world of the eye. What if architecture is created in pure silence? What if we draw, make models, create computer graphics or animations, all in a purely silent world of manipulations? Is there another word we could use instead of manipulations, which suggests the use of our hands? How do we transform with a silent eye, without the complicating acoustic chatter of desire? Words have wrought the world, while the eye has remained silent. There is a saying that suggests that our reach often exceeds our grasp. Words have no limits in what they can set in motion. The eye never sets anything in motion, a limpid pool of reflection. Could we let the eye set things in motion? Let us create with the eye. Let us create in silence.

8 PHOTOGRAPHER

searching the passing by
with lens for an inner eye
you seek to freeze
a nonchalant breeze
shaking a tall tree dry
the elusive search
for all that means much
within the edges of a frame
the mud-water slime
the dirt and the grime
speak qualities that define the why
tripping the shutter
with hardly a flutter
belies a tension-filled wait
the life in the gutter
the pompous old sitter
is what you call seeing it straight
till genius locus
automatic focus
you get it over in a flash

9 OLD MEN AND THE SEA

THE OLD MEN

the old men are still hanging around
they pop up in bus stop scraps of conversation
and are carried home
in paper bags of minds with market lists
they come forth at forked roads and railway stations
and moments when you are alone
they help out in far, far places
that prodigal sons have known
they witness scenes of jubilation
the prodigal's return has sown
they hide in cloaks of eternal fables
and are still around
in fluctuations and turns of tables
they always hold their ground
they surface with the turns of circles
they have their ups and downs
it matters not, their change of status
they are around
and around

THE SEA

the cape and the profound feeling of beyond
sails skimming seas
swells racing to hit the shore with a spray fist
surf splayed on rocks in a burst of joy - celebration and the pleasing
exhaustion of release
seaweed stench and the flowy floating froth
rivulets uncovering rocks with water lace and fountain beads
water gurgling in crevices in claustrophobic protest occasionally
blowing its top
bobbing up and down in boaty buoyancy
swirling salty sea mist stealing slowly across the sand
dreary dusk - the day drawing doors down to darkness

SEA BREEZE

the wind tousled the forest's hair
it shook away the seize
of the beat of heat
of sun replete
and refreshed with the breeze
the snores of doze
the slumber force
disappeared when the trees'
rustle of life
like notes of a fife
filled the air to please
the scraggy crag
the skimpy rag
brooded over the scene
till the rip of a burst
flicked the coat of dust
and both of them were clean
clean and fresh
of the noontime crush
by the daily gift of the seas

10 FROM EAST TO WEST

In the devout traditions of the West, the incarnation of the Word has a special place in the hearts of the people. Each self is seen as an incarnation, an assimilation, a series of epistemological bindings, and traces that progressively help the self to become. This devotion to incarnate the Word, to 'real'ize it in the flesh, has moved away to a world that instead tries to invoke the Word in the material, expending a vast amount of energy. As the West works more and more on this 'undertaking', the East is seeking to transcend the incarnations, assimilations, epistemological bindings and traces, in order to be pure in its agency. In the East, what has been built has to be transcended in order to be pure 'in the flesh.' Is this even possible? Elsewhere I have stated that particular actualization is a noble teleological goal. How can we be pure after particular actualization, so that the Word shines through us, unbound by any'thing'?

ABOUT THE AUTHOR

An architect by education and training, Ganapathy Mahalingam completed an undergraduate, professional education in Architecture at the School of Architecture and Planning in Chennai, India and became a registered architect in 1984. Ganapathy came to the United States in 1985 to pursue a Master's degree in Architecture, which he earned at Iowa State University in 1986. He taught computer-aided design at Iowa State University for a year before he returned to India to practice Architecture. He came back to the United States to complete a Ph.D. in Architecture at the University of Florida, which was awarded in 1995. Having spent half of his life in the culture of India, and half of his life in the culture of the United States, he has that balanced experience in life that spans the Old World and the New World. Currently educating future generations of architects at North Dakota State University, he is seeking to share...in the words of Le Corbusier...*les carnets de la recherché patiente...*

With diverse interests that range from philosophy, architectural design, computational modeling, Poetry, Music and Art, to culinary delights and travel, he has that strong curiosity to learn about the world around him, and wonders about all the things that remain to be discovered and done.

As a person who seeks to understand all the traditions that seek to understand, he is on a quest that is comprehensive, integrative and ultimately enlightening, in the sense of an experience in which all burdens are lifted. Another experience of enlightenment that he yearns for...is being awash in a light...that purifies the mind and rids it of accumulated traces...traces the ancients in India called *samskāra*...achieving the purity of freedom from all that is made!

He believes that this quest will be fulfilled when we all understand our own minds...in a single act of consciousness...foretold in the *Advaitic* tradition of India as...*tat tvam asi*...which he is bold enough to translate unconventionally as...abide in That!

www.ingramcontent.com/pod-product-compliance
Lightning Source LLC
Chambersburg PA
CBHW071941020426
42331CB00010B/2969